The Promise of Rust

THE PROMISE
OF RUST

Poems by

Hari Alluri

Mouthfeel Press

Jake,
in life, I believe in
seeking that which
gives you reason
to seek it again—
allow your fears
to teach you
passion
~Hari

Gratitude to the editors of the following journals, in which versions of these poems and fragments appear:

B O D Y Literature – "When you straggle..."

Five Quarterly – "We have here...," "I feel like I have to...," "Morning Collapses on the Bench," "I say this...," and "A chair speaks in riddles...," under the title "Refuse to Swim."

Toe Good – "Filth! You Filthy Piece of Trash, Whaddaap?!"

The Promise of Rust
Copyright © 2016 by Hari Alluri

Cover Art by Naomi Horii
Photograph by Vanessa Richards

Mouthfeel Press is an indie press publishing works in English and Spanish by new and established poets. We love innovative, experimental, contemporary forms, and engaging themes such as gender, sex, culture, language, folklore, spirituality, politics, art, and borderland issues. Our books are available through our website, Small Press Distribution, Amazon.com, at selected bookstores, or through authors' readings.

Contact information:
www.mouthfeelpress.com
Info-editor@mouthfeelpress.com

Published in the United States, 2015
ISBN: 978-0-9967247-3-9

M UTHFEEL PRESS

First Printing
Ten Dollars

TABLE OF CONTENTS

THE PROMISE OF RUST

GRATITUDES

Though so many more are crucial to my life and this work, *The Promise of Rust*—which was written primarily from Fall 2013-Summer 2014 on Kumeyaay land and Musqueam territory, whose keepers I give thanks—was directly helped into existence by the following:

Ancestors, blood and relation. Mom, Dad, Rina, Cyrill.
Lizz Huerta, whose love is why I was in the place this book could begin. Her family for welcoming me into their homes.
Avnika, Lucía, Kai, Raiden: welcome to the world. Mya, Paul, Ria: your growth amazing.
Cinder Block all ways. Cynthia Dewi Oka, Sevé Torres. David Maduli: so many drafts. Maritez, Zuzu & Apollo for lending me time. Miriam Ching-Louie.
Suheir Hammad: light. Chris Abani: the first key. Wayde Compton, Ross Laird. Juan-Felipe Herrera. Elmaz Abinader, Diem Jones, Cristina García: VONA, Las Dos Brujas.
Sandra Alcosser. Marilyn Chin. Piotr Florczyk. Ilya Kaminsky: method and form.
Poetic Youth. Poetry International. Jenny Minniti-Shippey: opportunity and gathering.
Locked Horn Press: co-builders.
My fellow SDSU MFA students: you're in this. Michael Luke Benedetto, Garrett Bryant, Karla Cordero, Kevin Dublin, Jesus Esparza, Dillon Scarzo for the extra curricular sessions on these poems specifically.
For allowing me to bother you with early drafts of these poems: Jas Gill, Cyrus Tasalloti, Erik Haensel, John Fillmore, Makita Desilets, Fayza Bundalli. Naomi Horii, the book cover is the smallest part.
Lizz Huerta—so many versions and visions: bless our balcony.
Mouthfeel Press, Maria Maloney: thank you for believing in the work.

My future, my very mother, my far horizon,
Into your light, into your breadth and height, into my fright,
I abandon myself

—Henri Michaux

THE PROMISE OF RUST

Here, he said, sun.

And he said it like soda pop cans, like the downpour
on streetlights we love.

Then we have a bus line steeped in kindness and trolley
cruelty. The earth spins. Something clogs. Bare feet
teach streets the heavy lifting of beautiful women,
non-virginal laughter to a boy at fifteen (a boy who feels
himself as thin as his baptism thread). Teach evening
how city is at odds with night, how we must work
with the wind to free ourselves from the wind, while
years subside, more armored, more delicate. Like trees,
I don't know quite what the shape of a bow resembles,
but it's close.

Tell me, are there bright and spacious neighborhoods and suburbs who hide their alleys? Are there desert animals in the rainforest town?

In one place the city seems to shrink around the blanketed elephant river swallowing its tails, a disturbance of teenage boys launching cat howls and roman candles.

*

Every generation wishes for itself
a better mop. Face on, out to strain.
And the water boiling coffee
steeping time is best for dish-wash,
but the blur of it, the herky-jerk
injury of glass on tap.

In a Time of War,

a woman who kills
and cannot bring herself to kill.

The war has changed this valley's shape—this grass
beside a woman's lungs.

In a time of war.

And the streets
are at odds with a woman's calloused feet.

In a time of war a woman beside
the animal she eats.

The hunter is the one who kills
and who cannot bring herself to kill.

All the streets of a country
watch: a woman turns in their sleep.

When it rained, the city was in
its anecdotes, the wars that soaked through
a worm between a rice paddy and a fishing hook.

*

I strike a match across my memory of his face, feed it
to kindling for the night's fire. My match is the reflecting
light of a downtown window's glint on this cloud of exhaust.

Boats await inside open windows for the flood to come
along, the eventual fear of staying anywhere but here.

Tell me, in what language would you have me try?

On another day when I was younger, I was in a country
where the trolley lines trick cars into making left turns
they didn't mean. Another boy, who comes from a place
I will never visit, taught me to spit with the wind behind me.
What trolleys know, our infinite capacity to sit broadside
and stare straight forward, noting only the unimportant.

A Song

God, please refuse to sing
the song you sang
after you stopped

being a butter thief—
grant this burglar
the archery of your voice.

Give ear to the low hum in the trees.
Give ear and besiege.
The shape of an ear, listening to itself.

*

There's an old man complaining, "You want to be fed
again? You're a pain in the ass, stupid cat." Do I love it?
I don't know.

Sensations converse between the sharp and smooth,
of turmeric, of coconut oil, mustard seed, the milky
heaving of fantasy breasts from the stovetop heat. Garlic
cloves, I mean: my fingertips ruffled by their skin.

Then there's a boy with his Fanta Orange warming to a
syrup the consistency of grog. And the grog passed around
in a bowl by the older men. And their laughter at his face
when one uncle lets the nephew get in on the bowl.

I have trouble with all this coffee shop, this lack of stray
dogs. I feel like calling anyone when it's cold, but not when
carpets are scarce. You have to save some yogurt curdling
bacteria for the next round.

I am writing to you from a barstool on 3rd Street.
You must see this: the trees do not tremble.
They have a ridiculous number of taps.
Some people here have stories for veins.
Between us, the dancing of bartenders calling on their
smiles every time they face our way.
Whenever one changes a keg, I notice a well dressed
patron on the end of the bar I gender as a woman
mouth a prayer. I count the seconds it takes.
The barkeep returns too soon to have unshot the line,
and I shove off offended.

Nearby, in the phosphorescence, soldiers pick their teeth
with egrets, orca try to wash off oil-slicked gulls,
drones have their homing devices installed.

Honoring their own story, trains carry flies
from one edge of a subcontinent to the other.

Too Many Teeth Surround His Tongue

My friend used to shit-talk tons to morning,
dumpster, alley, park, to coffee-stained light,
to nicotine, to knuckles, losing his breath

those hours when blood plows hungry
down the two-toke parking lot and through
impending ambiance. He commanded

and I—I watched. Stepping ginger
in the wet socks of his high, he shouts up
the walls, "Everything's a quarry,

dammit! But how many hustles are human, truly?"
and he grimaces because the bass hit us low.
Wary of repetition, of my rhyme-scheme breaking

down at Ashwin's return, I rewind my tinted windows
to pester a small rain. The opening in that man:
his yearning to arrange our grief

according to the rules for a gangster mix. Each drink
he takes is a ploy. The bass yells, "more than
its actual strength, the causes he pours it in,

like a booming system lining a hooptie." He confessed
and sighed from all the angles of a butterfly knife.
Inside his forehead: our city river's sawdust flow

mixed with some neon London. It loosened
like he was visiting, and he was. Our cry—silent
as the laughter crazing inside the next bottle.

I love dirt too, people who question
the nation because of what their tracks
betrayed. I have smiled up at a flag,
recognizing in its gentle
sway the violence I fear most. A poet claps,
"I won't kiss your fucking flag." And I smile.

We remember own language can never be enough for
the love that's here, only all of them, all of them at once,
the way it must have sounded at the beginning, and I cling
to the languages I've lost with the one that clings to me:

rock cemetery fossil jack move stolen car land perfect
pool game sex on the beach in the kitchen at the movies
on the jungle floor in flight descending linked under water
jackals and parakeets bird of paradise raccoons in
the basement kleenex pushing toes apart nail polish super
hero lucha libre ceremony discord speak manifesto speak
guilt speak filth steel girder fly trap onilé capsfull of 151
peaty scotch a slurp of cola fur pelts and sneering watches
orthodox om nama shit sun all of them joined at the same
speech in the silence dirt bahala na surrendering silence.

But your combination of treble and consonant engages
the start of my blood into blood—a turn on image into
image—seduction by image. We haven't always gilded
like this, but. And we cling to the languages we've lost
the ones that cling to we.

These boats like a prison wall.
The crew's iron cage is limber
hinges oiled to shut more clean.
And here the fragile gesture
in an opening fist amen.

*

A short turn moon between cumulus drift. The ring of it
permeates steady and shabash upon this layered vault.

There are subterranean disturbances, too. These small
avenues, perpendicular to where things go down, dark.
This recycled rain, this recycled rain, this rain
peoples the entire sky with its blanket of affectation.

"Filth! You Filthy Piece of Trash, Whaddaap?!"

Later, he ducked off to piss. The propaganda
I miss most: raps on our pager greetings,
diminished for melody. Our inside jokes
are now this jersey dank against my skin,
yet another language I falter every couple years.

The day he left us was a pebble of a snail
making its way from the barbecue
underside. We drunk-walked the blocks
between avenues, looking for that sign
we promised each other we would steal.

We see nothing, except what is so pleasing to see. Traffic lights stuck on blinking red, their shelter meant to shelter nothing but themselves. An embossment of pickle juice spilled in the fridge. The unmade bed's vacated chorus, falsetto.

Childhood's bottles
and cans commemorate the walls.

*

This is the ruddy smile at the bottom of a glass of
powdered milk. This is the barroom mirror in which you
talk to yourself. These are your gutshot eyes smiling
with whiskey and heavy with resistance to tomorrow's
alarm. And yet, time is the same for slug and hummingbird
and the hungover ornament stuck between them.

I bleed like a goat's voice and leave the room unswaddled.

What Is Time

A barber in his cups,
danger-filled as any soldier.
His unkempt dog
noses the air for smoke.
A dog who drags its tongue for blood
on the day's shavings. Time,
a dog who just will not sit still.

The sound of liquid leaving
bottle for mouth is peace.

*

I picture a hunter's smile like mine. I'm three. My father
returns. I'm hugging his leg, cheek to his bony knee. I lean
back to shout up my excited hands for the toy he brandishes
above my head. My cheeks ache with joy like an old man
complaining, "you're a pain in the ass, cat." It's how
he gives thanks.

We have here a dog, harbour voiced, lashed off hungry.
An uncastable vessel, it arrives under duress of real boats,
this dog.

Then we have a dog and three things to do, like wind in a
desert we pray to, its bones stuck in a dog's drying throat.

I feel like I have to, he said, to hold to the language of one empire in face of another. At night the arriving ships bellow like whalesong in a cactus' sap where you are.

Morning Collapses on the Bench,

lights up a joint. A stoning to get rid of the war,
and the four of us try to take on the elbows of
a cross, which is in its Hindu symbol incarnation
on the front of a house. We are reaching toward
four—suspended, free—dots, like Holi, but dirty:
morning, the city, seagull, and I.

The smell of ants being born surrounds us—the serenity in constant work, a stream's whitewater aspirations, without protection. It's not the same as the fog from above: higher tide, skyscrapers for buoys.

*

The Language I Lost

Every time someone weeps,
a poem in English.

I write in the plaza—aerograms—light a cigarette,
jab it down. Sometimes coffee breath, sometimes
beer. Writing, I forget I smoke while I claw

into the good paper. Stripped to cruelty
is good paper, and the smoke spine above the bench
resolves into a clarinet.

There are clouds, fingers of orange, ink
to lose in every swish. I smoke
a lot, write even more. Whisper,

"this heaven we invented leaves
and leaves not enough room for darkness."
I mail the letters, by setting them on fire—

Being a stranger to both desert and temperate, to the streets in every town I find myself, the thing I most truly know is an undershirt shrunken so it never quite stays tucked in. Vexation, so I pull this sweater hood over my hair to cover my ears and neck.

*

And even the gentlest marching is an act of violence.

I say this with a signal light's urge to lose its job. I think
of you like a tequila bottle to the lips, the hot springs'
fumes drinking down stars. I would say other things
if I wanted to be kind.

You gather gestures in a basket and they escape.

*

A chair speaks in riddles and a table's
denial is flat. But the footstool is honest:
even when it's stored away, it yearns to break down.
The lockpick work of thieving death from death,
while tilapia meat begins to glow in the pan.

NOTES

The Promise of Rust is part of a longer project that meditates on and offers interpolations of Henri Michaux's "I Am Writing to You from a Far-off Country."

"In a Time of War" transposes elements of Tadeusz Różewicz, Adonis and Muhammad Al-Maghut.

"Give ear..." is after Christopher Okigbo.

"Balconies, Scarves and Daggers" is after Zbigniew Herbert's "The Rain," with elements transposed from Alexander Blok.

"Houses circled..." is for Tomás Harris.

"We have here..." is after Paul Celan.

"Morning Collapses on the Bench, Lights Up a Joint" is after Edip Cansever.

"The language I Lost" is for Mohsen Emadi.

AUTHOR'S BIOGRAPHY

Photo by Vanessa Richards

Hari Alluri is a co-founding editor of Locked Horn Press, a community facilitator, and a poet. His work appears in *B O D Y, Chautauqua, Contemporary Verse 2, Poetry International, Word Riot* and *Dismantle* (Thread Makes Blanket). He is the author of *Carving Ashes* (CiCAC).